AF614971

LIPS

lips

poems by

Pete Hoida

Allison and Busby, London

First published in 1972 by
Allison & Busby Limited, 6a Noel Street, London W.1

SBN 85031 067 9

Printed in Great Britain
by Latimer Trend & Co. Ltd,
London & Whitstable.

ACKNOWLEDGEMENTS

Some of these poems were previously published in the following: *The Children of Albion* (Penguin), *Contrasts, Cyclops, Earthship, Gnosis, How, Lon Chaney, Doves for the Seventies* (Corgi), *Mandate, New Departures, Notting Hill Herald, Pause, Plexus, Poetmeat,* BBC Radio London, *Second Aeon, Skylight, Solstice, Tlaloc.*

CONTENTS

THE EARLY POEMS

VISION

There's a 1/6d. cinema,
a shop called Kaddish,
even smells of Ginsberg's casbah
and garbage pails.
Tall corrugated tin bins,
lids shields against stolen railing
thrown by hole in trouser boy.
Screaming tricycles and melons,
lettuces and ripe negroes,
stripe shirt,
and others proud walking.
It's gay and sad and rich enough!

STAFFIN

Waves lash,
brown red shrubs walk close to the ground.
Showers in uprights
merge
and join the sea and sky
in grey,
to hide the islands
mountain tops and
beat the brown red shrubs closer to the ground.

ALONE

I did not see her.
They told me she had left.

We went to a cafe.
The others left,
one by one.
We were together in the cafe.
We were alone in the cafe.
We were alone together in the cafe.

(I thought I would write to you.
Everything I write is for you.)

SONG

I have a small room
in a small town
. . . out the window, trees
      in the afternoon
      black and naked
      in the morning
      the fine tracery
      of branches
      patterned
    on my wall
    night and the wind
    towing the moon
    over Cleeve Hill
and yet the skies are too complex
(I do not seek an answer
for there is no question
other than the centre
which I am surely approaching).

WINTER

Winter: listened to the rain
and went to the corner shop
and sometimes I smoked
and heard Parker for hours.
People came and left
and I thought about writing a poem
about winter
and never made it to the typewriter.

Parker improves all the time
and I prime a white canvas
which is my mind this winter
and do not paint it
for three days   beautiful,
which is a square white square
and seems a pity to spoil it.
So I never made it to the typewriter
and sometimes the corner shop
smoked heard Parker and rain.

I had no despair
and met someone who liked
orange/lime green/Sibelius,
but we never made it
and there were other
young girls sadly impossible.

And now a confusion of feelings,
a chaos of vagaries
warmer nights once again
and a compulsion of comparisons.

I look out the window:
a nostalgia of little green leaves
and your body
I would kiss you again and again
and lean with you out
this window
where I see a confusion of pipes
the arteries of lives and houses,
coveys of bins and tin sheds
and dead bikes,
the colour of waste,

expressed by my arab radio
that makes strange sounds
far into the night for me,

a melange of cultures
Arab, Italian and popship
in which we are deeply travelled
dig you/it/like summer
but you are not here
so I dig it
and all things
and am warmly nostalgic for
the spring myth and you
that are not yet arrived/have been
under street lights
in a quiet town.

"HOW'S THE CLIMATE OLD BEEN?"

the rain pissing in the trees
the trees pissing in the rain
the pissing rain in the trees
the trees in the pissing rain
the rain in the pissing trees
the pissing trees in the rain

SEAGULLS

Seagulls, white blades in the air,
fish swim, fly from rock,
a stone perch, a few fuzzy grasses
their spiky heads stuck up above the level eye.
— The sky bluer than postcards, the sea
a better poem than composed
by any 'poet'; can you give me reason
for that? The moon pulling this way
wants such for splits in these gigantic rocks.
The same concrete thoughts whisked from your head
by the same gulls/fish fly over
the brim horizons of your understanding
        your estimations of nature
        your locations
of stone
        outcrops of rock.
        Hard images.

        Equations mother don't satiate
the bitter lands of reason
like these cries;
the taste on my lips,
the mist coming over the hill,
the hazy waters of the sun settle on the sill.

This lava loosed hot on the land
big monuments
        to what taste you wish,
your haste to 'understand' maybe.
I ask you only hear.
The post colours the gull's belly
your reasoning like that steep cliff

at the end there
many mosses growing on it,
fuzzy green grey,
you crystallize moss in words,
hear birds.
Ferns creeping up the bank,
orange flowers shoot through them
to the sky, past your mind's horizon,
the location of this lot, hot on the footprints
of my translations.

The sea spray is delicate and cool
compared with that;
from the rock you stand on
which moves,
the sea or you?
The sky?

The one reflected in the other,
simple things demanding simple words
(seaweed is washed here and there,
no more to it
lest you see messages
there's no one way grain
to these million stone eggs here beneath
your feet.
The wind that takes your hair
bears no significance.
There is glass and concrete and machine
and atom,
let not these detract from here/now
let these words be the short endings to long abstractions
when there is only sea,
small spiders bumbling through fuzzy grasses
and a fly buzzing.

At night, the mist coming over
the rock headland
        over the bay the dull orange
        electric sun,
        without hard edges,
        muzzy and orange hanging there in the grey,
no horizon
        only the two tones of grey and the orange
then just below
        waves crashing about in gullies.
very
        steep down there.
Perched by a rock,
nearer to your nose
        lichens and small grasses, and small spiders
        scurrying here and there in no apparent patterns.

You leave the poem to go out
chase the cows from the porch,
the sea floating in the window
— I mean the sound always —
and a fly buzzes around the white room
        butterflies chase each other
        like inseparable twins
        with invisible threads —
the landscape of your understanding
and the sea
                the same.

CRISTOBEL

O Cristobel/spirit the dead ferry talks
over sea/eyes sparkling
dark blue waves dancing, the sad spirits of understanding.

Houses squatted in little groups
tiny on hill brow far away
the sound of the sea/no bird cries
faint buzzing of a fly, the tenuous lines of association

between the landscape of your 'Understanding'
and this granite sculpture/sticking
its great black back into the sky
humped up there/the purple of the heather
showing on the nearer and lower slopes.

Tiny telegraph poles conveying what messages
across these hills
like "good morning mrs brown and hallo there,
hallo –"

nearer the ferns reaching the edge of the cliff/
the grasses and flowers stretching
from under you –
                                        you have surveyed in a few
lines
this white room and the buzzing of the fly
to the far distance and the implications
of telegraph communications –
"hallo there, hallo, mrs brown?"
O Cristobel/spirit the dead ferry talks.

DID YOU EVER SEE THOSE PERSIL CLOUDS

Did you ever see those Persil clouds
sailing up the madonna blue sky,
no thoughts streaked across your mind,
no places to go in dreams of orange and purple,
no prissy strangers to stick outcrops of rock
in your gentle landscapes,
no characters
like the orange butterflies settling on the blue plants
into the distant photograph,
no position to prosody the landscape of
stone flowers and sea,
no neon eternity camp in your mind's eye,
no window for thoughts to stream
across the landscape, mother
your equations kindle
no doubts in my mind.

MORLON STRODE

Into the utter white mist
dancing like rocks and mud,
into the tide,
through marshes,
past seagulls,
past sportsmen
shooting flying ducks,
Morlon strode..

COFFEE ON THE BALCONY

The haze rising off the wet morning,
the first sunshine raining through
the wet green leaves
the balcony . . .
                    with coffee
or how it could be
listening to the singing
of the day,
if it weren't for the crossfire
of you shooting your wife,
her shooting you.

THE SILENT SPACEMAN

No scale to the soft breathing,
nicely from the bottom of the stomach now
like the air from a balloon maybe . . .
the network of trees again,

the sparse sparse forests of laziness,
to dry deserts;
those were places
I went on ships
as well.

Listen to the falling
of scaffolding,
the buses on afternoons
. . . . hear a caged bird sing.

The stuff of the earth,
the cold air into the coppice,
larch and birch;

a scarecrow warbles,
a gull pecks a worm
in a brown ploughed field.

JOURNEYMAN TO APPRENTICE

I plunder our night with my words,
and come back;
                    'mountains laden with meaning:—'
"And in the Japanese film   the doors slid sideways,
they entered with a glide.
    In England, the door, wHoosh, open
    wide."
and she sighed.
"Oh well, I suppose they all live in prefabs
  now."
and she laughed.

The echo down this valley.

The snow, the questions,
                    laden with meaning
each with a sigh.
The logs, the skies, the animals,
                    the mountain retreats
into a list
distant as my memory.

MAD BEN

up there – on the tops of hills
– cots wolds – thin grey air
the thorn – the grey clouds scudding
across the wet brown earth –
the grey green grass –
mute sheep – scattered and looking
by gates at you –
                                        bullocks old
as England peering out of
eternally decaying buildings –
the roofs sloping into the grass
falling
into the land – and these big wet
pools of shit and water and upturned
grass and root – sodden bales of hay –
dead hedges and grey stone walls
dissecting the distance and the small
bands of trees
tall beech – lady like – green limbed –
stalking in thin lines across
the distance – then few maybe
two   three spruce or larch on
hillocks – the incredible deadness
of winter – and the aliveness of the
deadness and the wet slanting
rain on your cheek – the grey
clouds scudding low across the
landscape – throwing brief patches of
mist your way and rising – then the
thin light of winter's
sun appears –

The visitant appears
around the cottage corner –
we disappear into
the edge of the canvas –
there are short rubbing noises

SNAP

write the photo:
bridge across estuary   to spit
        yellow sand on other side
railway to one side of walk
clear as shivering flakes of rust
gravel spilling off the edge
        into river
cardboard mountains in golden sun
the galleon   the lone gull
your nose eyes rich mouth
greedy for detail
wouldn't meet mine
        antik lingering
asides
        each measured moment
halted in a snap
cold wind   streaking cloud
near lowering sun
Gothic mansion on the bank
simplicity the absence of many things
How Often SUCH an Absence!
half way across bridge
clarity of face
white boat with red line
oatmeal brown and cardboard hill
standing papier mâché vision
of 4 o'clock winter in wales

MY LADY RIDES OUT

The rod maybe golden
    and needs to be broken
across his back,

his need
the sum of your lack.
"Friend, the road is long
the purpose obscure,
would you measure even this
by your father's scale?"

Driving my vision
    like a nail
into the dawn,
pulling floods out of the sun,
quenching the moon's thirst,
that is my song.
I slaughter small enemies
and praise queens,
    with equal ease
– the vision escapes –
the fish-hook gleams,
my lady rides out
in a funeral limousine.

DREAM

My father ran laughing
into the bright yellow cornfield.
He lay on his back
and disappeared in the tall stems
and took in the immensity
of the blue sky.
And the road was clear
and gold
and he was, strangely, simply, old
and innocent,
laughing as I handed him
a ripe plum
I stole.

THE FIELD, THE EMPTY FLAGPOLE AND THE ROPE

Part 1

To get the wispy
rushes
      on the paper
cool as the dew,

the daffodil cliff
      and the riff,
the white/slate grey
      cottage
all done better in a painting
by (   ), he said,
that's not me.

The mist shining about you,
those gull cries no more,
the ocean lapping gently
      on the shore,
and all this kale.

Not a single snap here,
drifting like mist
      blown steadily
from the sea
      and you on the promontory
waiting for a signal
      as I sail off
      to the sound of a
      rope slapping against
      the empty flagpole.

Part 2

Gnats in the
early morning sun
bumbling around the
empty translation
of spring.

My mechanism rockets
into the blue, leaving
an empty shell on the rock.

    Watching a little tree
in the garden change
golden to green;
    time lingers patient and ancient
in the stone walls.

A lizard snaps
at the gnats, is stopped
on the slab,
        stillness:

a cock crows
a dog barks into the empty sky.

Part 3

Battered cedars and an
old stone house in the
  clear light of dawn.
A swan flies into the
  blue, a
    crake calls,
the pigs are shewed into
  the estover,
the goat is eating the
  golden flower of this
  furze.

Piscary, watercress and the
riff of an old wheel
turns on this,
  the bracken
broken and big stone slabs
  of eternity
that make little fields
  where the goat is tied
its darkest night.
  The wind making its runes
in the raggy ash and pine.

Part 4

Out onto the porch
under the full moon
in the empty field,
and back to the empty
            house,

waiting
for someone
to arrive.

QUARTET

FARMER'S ADVICE

Seagulls, cowpads;   and nothing says the farmer
"whitewash the walls,"   he finally says.

Old ash   by remains   of old house,
fields mad with foxgloves,

thistle and sorrel and
nettles   into the stony distance there

THE SHED

Two days   most all of the time
moving things   in and out.
Finally discard   the mirror,
few little purple flowers on windowsill.

Paint the front door   clear blue,
after removing some dead animal claws
from it   of some previous tenant's
magic.

I wonder who   that strange tenant was?

VISITOR IN LANDSCAPE

The red sorrel   when you pull
the seeds drip   through your hands,
the iris, furze;   a few brown cows
one yellow field   full with flowers

another of   green/silver   edged blades.

Went to a farmhouse   to see some people
it was empty   they were out.
Tadpoles in the warm part   of a slow stream
wriggling about   waiting to become frogs

hop into the distance and spawn.

Few old stones, ditches, paths
no one there; a few addressed,
unopened   letters

MOONSHOT

From each low scattered rolling hill
can see the next or the last
or another.Ship on the deep blue sea
passing to France.

In the farmyard scattered abandoned toys
and all the old scatty iron machinery
of agriculture layed rusting.

The highways for tourists (the fish all
go to the central market,
and back down again.

Newspaper reports the moonshot,
flinging those expensive suits away!
But coming back
having grabbed those precious scoops
of moondust and rock!
"o foolish slaves, o wicked masters"

Back here we are into the future
afore; the rotting cars of commerce
old wheel shafts and battered axles in the mud
while scruffy children run amongst.

CODA

little ship on deep green sea
little bird in pale blue sky

            mare and foal
   rabbit stoat
foxglove orchid
daisy dandelion
      string
crow
      rook flower
sun shower

little ship on deep green sea
little bird in pale blue sky

MEMORY (for Ken Cox)

Space was your station,
all premises/pointers
            noted as such
—that was often,
        and more than,
            your stance.

The trip you kept
      months in a drawer
"it's all over now . . . ."

a fragrant tune in a faded room,

and I'm guessing
        heavens and hells bigger than that
causing the classic
blink,
      as if that secret could/unsurety would
be
   displaced
              so easily.

Images hatch like flies
but you came down the way
   like a dash/thus
        in the mind.

AUTUMN

Shot with visions of   concrete smoke
equally white   up the sky;
once again   it is autumn.
Sitting   always with you
silently in railway carriages   and cracking.
The plane sailing surely across the pane   and through
the next

a bloody tear from the eye,   a bell hanging,
the question loose . . . .
tracks bending gracefully   (into the distance)

POLITICS

A still dank deep green wood,
or two, re-forested with this gesture,
the yellow and red flames
licking dangerously from the warning sign;
a burst of bickering guns rang out.

In the second wood
a shiny motor car
sat glinting darkly
on the path. No
sign nor body,
yet so white and new
signifying only perhaps
seduction.

MUSEUM

Outside, a silly statue
Called fortitude,
Inside, Bosch, Goya,
All heaven and hell
Let loose;
But the audience are bored,
They are so much part of it –
They are only there
Because they think they ought to be

IDEA

The curiously inept
Idea of enjoying a poem
As if it were like a good sausage;
From the university of despair I go
To loss upon glad loss

MOROCCO

Lux Blanco, Lever Maroccain Incorporated;
A wash after the journey,
Carefully provided by I.C.I.,
A tooly bar of white soap,
And all its laborious consequences.
But the tiles are real,
Our hotel a cool chessboard
In maroon and green.
And they have assimilated
The best and most significant
Of our culture,
I thought, sitting opposite
Bar Ray Charlie Sandwich.

THE STANCE

The dream, is not the poem,
It is previous to waking

With someone else's voice
In the throat, and knowing
At that moment you're about
To break into voice,
Only of that person you are
As much as, seeing me dance
You have, resultantly, a stance.

THERE IS NOTHING IN IT

There is nothing in it;

you go in
sit down
and drink a cup of tea.

I cannot find a relevance
in this situation,
other than, thirst.

The date, the time
and the place
are for you, to provide.

The train, of course,
leaves soon
and, although we don't have to,
we think we must, catch it.

Otherwise we would sit here
drinking tea.
And this in itself could be important,
if one failed to remember,
those previous instances.

AFTER THE FAST

And it could be, wasn't, didn't, is not.
All the loveliest negative affirmations
furl under his tucked wing
which spans the yellow house.

Photographs of possible affinities
in the album, by the outhouse,
brought it in, put it down,
invisible, on the carpet
making its debut, swelling enormously, proportionally
in the early turbulence of air.

FOUND POEM

apes
baboons
lemurs
woolly indri
Goeldi's monkey
swamp monkey

aye aye

THREE

Lovely things
are happening

the sun is falling

Goodnight, sun

cloud slur

fir barn

(delete)

FOUR

Pick up a sliver
cloud slurr

horror beauty factories
slouch

FAIR BAIRN

It's late
and Don Quixote is going to bed

switch off the stars
lie on your back

chug sludge
awa
o'er the brown hills
Esso bitumen lists

LOVE'S COUNTRY

Yes, Tom
tomorrow we'll go
to the airport,

it will be 10.53
a.m. exactly

"When England Rose"
a tight sliver of dawn

and we'll photograph
the waitresses, les sandwiches.

AMONGST ALL THE WILDE FLOWERS

In like kind;
a withered crone,
        burnt fur
over the village
museum,
        a beeste.

St. Senera, after the mermaid,
and all the dogs of Zennor Churchtown,
                                                        sniff.

A small rabbit from Brownsville
shone across the lithe space;

the winter of Tennyson's
biography
        said,

turning his bulbous eyes,
that goat,
        such sacrificial pomp,

a big white dam.

All tortured toothpaste
and chances to win
a fibreglass sailing boat.

His Sundays

sink into
the eyes
        of a giant lady-bird

self-conscious in his
red and black
velvet skin

amongst all the wilde flowers

Burnt holly, driftwood
and wrappers,

the moonflower's
childhood

and active guilt

to the high yowl
of rooks from a cornstack.

The farm machinery tacks
blue polythene pig-feed
across the
low black soil.

UNTITLED

And staying here,
    The Virgin And The Gypsy,

all next week.

    Hallo peanut,
    tennis boots,
    humility;
    the rock climber hangs on.

All the pieces of
    this weeks jig
    saw on true love
    cellophane teardrop,
    American t.v.

    And buy a new notebook
    full of asterisks,
    his star-sign.

CAROLINE

The girl's thigh shines
in mid-air
    whilst the white sofa
    continues over the bridge,

she whispers soft
o softer lip.

We eat a real Spaghetti Napolitan

and love comes in
on the bald periphery
of this main new rising thing

as we go into a room
as warm as a glowing tomato

and Rubens says Hello,
                    and everything

ARRIVE BACK 9.45 PM

FROM STARK PERSUASION

Black softwoods and
ruined silver

slavering for dawn

nether grief in a
        little revolver

with lace about
his ruff
and neck of wind

a kind of red sign
that you find by
a lighthouse or airstrip

and white

blocked

11.30 p.m.   (guess

A match,
        phosphor   RED   GREEN   BLUE,

the break of day –

a murmer approaches   'my eye'

the star in the cascade in the box
I give you

BELLS

"Starry chicken Kiev
delicious noodles"
                    (ex-count Dracula's

POST-CARD

from Dirk.

A soft smash;

the denial,
the crest,

I give you what gems
the squall   the Tempest,

A garland of rubber bullets,
and teeth

borne on the wings
of the Financial Times Index

LIFE

his badly worn cloak.

Explicit, terrific
and humorous

WINGS and FLAPS and RUDDERS

"to get back"

her slender Cirrus Cumulus

A bachelor of science

"FRESHWATER POLLUTION"

not scarce,

but sparse

and "rigged with intention"

LOST CITY

The stars "turn"
and dawn "comes up"

When "This, the happiest hour of my life
is filled with tear-stained notes"

I write.

A voice that hears me
with a long milky throat sips

"You charlatan".

She rings up ten times a day
TO BE RELEASED so I make her
(my favourite tune;

maps

that I am just off

the edge of

and flying

back into the kitchen chair

that has 'THE WHEEL OF EXISTENCE'

hung in the struts.

THE DAUGHTERS OF WARM RAIN

"I will buy a mountain
and call it Rubber Scuta,
Pear Halves in Heavy Syrup,
The Lovely Grip of The Butt of Lewis."

Shall I talk of gneiss
or Protestant Harris?

or the bus to the Back Area –

depart Stornoway 9.30 p.m.
arrive Back 9.50 p.m.
depart Back 10.00 p.m.
arrive Stornoway 10.20 p.m. :

we'll go into the south,
Aye,
        & Mystical Rose   will glisten.

A smudge of pink moss
in the Gazette or armpit;

"The fishing declined after
the First World War
with the coming of the Zulus"

not a strange tribe but a long
wooden boat with lapping strips;

and the sun stays up late.

But the butcher from Laxdale
brings the papers,

not the daughters of warm rain,
nor the heady fronds of meadow sweet,
but Marathon, the Peanut Choc Bar.

I roll up my heavy eye
in the lily that floats
from Eye Head Loch;

– she had to walk to Toe Head
& was back by two in the morning.